# Simply Scru .
# Southern Sweets

Patricia B. Mitchell

Revised Edition

*Published 1991 by the author at the Sims-Mitchell House Bed & Breakfast, P. O. Box 429, Chatham, VA 24531.*
*Tel/fax: 804-432-0595*
*E-mail: answers@foodhistory.com*
*Website: www.foodhistory.com*

*Printed in the U. S. A.*
*ISBN 0-925117-39-0*

*Seventh Printing, June 1999*

*- Illustrations -*

*Front Cover -* **Scene of the Crime**, *by Henry H. Mitchell.*

*Inside Title Page -* **Circumstantial Evidence**, *by Henry H. Mitchell.*

*Inside Back Cover - portrait of the author by David L. Mitchell.*

*Back Cover - provided by Dover Publications, Inc., New York.*

# Table of Contents

\* \* \* \* \* \* \* \* \* \* \* \* \* \* \* \* \* \*

# Preface

Analyze this collection of recipes, and I think you'll find five influences, "streams of Southern sweetness," you might say. First, there are nostalgic family recipes as prepared at home (in my childhood) or sampled at family reunions. Next are foods found on dessert tables at church potluck suppers and dinners on the grounds. Third are traditional Southern foodways rediscovered during the back-to-the-land movement of the 1960's and 1970's. Then come the exuberantly sensual treats from the Gulf Coast reflecting the Louisiana motto "Let the good times roll!" Last, you will find the prudent approach of the health-conscious 1980's. — And if you think there is any contradiction in putting all these together, well, Honey, that's just the way Southern cooking is — a joyous synthesis of ideas and recipes!

- Patricia Mitchell
Chatham, Virginia

\* \* \* \* \* \* \* \* \* \* \* \* \* \* \* \* \* \*

# Introduction

As I was growing up, my parents and I lived with my maternal grandfather Charlie Jones in Dry Fork, Virginia. Charlie's eating habits (he wouldn't let me or the other grandchildren call him granddaddy or such because it made him feel old) reflected an earlier time. He thrived on milk, butter, cheese, fresh vegetables, salt-rising bread, beef, fish, and poultry. He did not eat a lot of desserts, although his favorite was sweet potato pie, and he loved peppermint patties. This was a well-known fact, and at Christmas he received boxes of them.

He also sucked Sens-sens. These were tiny, mysterious-looking, chalky, olive green-colored square breath-fresheners which, as I recall, came in a small tan envelope. Their flavor was vaguely clove-like. He kept his supply in a wardrobe in his bedroom. (When I could find nothing else to feed my sweet tooth, I occasionally sampled some of his Sens-sens.) From this slim bit of evidence, you can guess that I adored sweets. — My other dining habits were quite different from Charlie's, too.

A typical lunch for me included two or three moon pies (as many as Mom would let me eat). That was dessert, of course, but I'm listing things in order of importance. Ideally, a Royal Crown Cola (an "R. C.") accompanied this repast. The main course was a bologna sandwich. (Preferably the bologna was heated first in a skillet with butter . . . . ) Peanut butter sandwiches were another yummy possibility. The optimum side dish was a mountain or two of potato chips, and if everything was perfect, this fine meal was served on a wiggly metal TV tray in the den as the *Bob Cummins Show* or *Ann Southern* (I don't remember the spelling) or *Sky King* or another personality illuminated the screen and my mind (?).

But back to sweets: I was passionate for chocolate. In the years of loose and missing teeth, Milky Ways were my desire, although Mom's favorite, Baby Ruth, was an excellent choice when chew-power was available. With a full set of chompers, peanut brittle was also fabulous; and chocolate-covered cherries always sent me into happy sugar euphoria. As time passed and the nickname "Fat Pat" was heard (not as bad as a lot of jokes about my last name, Beaver!), I tried to control my plump little body's lust for food, doling out special treats to myself. (I'd take half a dozen cubes of sugar out to Gunsmoke, my horse, and only personally eat a few cubes. I would buy a milk chocolate Hershey bar and methodically nibble the squares, attempting to make the bar last through *Route 66*. TV star George Maharis ["Buzz Murdock"] was certainly enough to make me want to be slim and attractive!)

Holiday time bought special food temptations. Not only did Christmas giving result in Charlie's receiving peppermint patties, which he passed around, but there was also Mama's commendable ice box fruitcake, Aunt Ethel's irresistible pound cake, and various cookies and candies which appeared on the scene. (Halloween was usually too much of a good thing treat-wise. I got more sick than satisfied with all that candy.) Valentine's might also bring forth a box of chocolates — hurrah! Easter, though, was my favorite food event. Hollow chocolate bunnies went down the hatch (to my tummy) ears first, and I craved the black and red jelly beans. (The pastel-colored beans and marshmallow-type eggs did not send me into ecstasy.) Something about spring seemed to prompt chocolate giving, though, — oooo, all those martyred candy rabbits!

And what about now? What desserts and sweets fill the bill, as far as I'm concerned? I'm still a chocoholic, though I limit my intake of non-nutritious foods these days. However, when I splurge, I want fudge or Charlie Brown ice cream (chocolate and peanut butter) or something very chocolatey. The Caribbean Room of the Pontchartrain Hotel on St. Charles Avenue in New Orleans flaunts a dieter's downfall — Mile High Pontchartrain Pie, a crust stacked with layers of ice cream, topped with a tall crown of meringue, and covered with chocolate sauce. My, oh, my! Let's hope that modern medical research discovers that sugar and chocolate are actually healthful!

Other desserts intersperse the "chocolate occasions," though, and they are also tempting enough to get lyrical about — but enough words! Let's get on to some scintillating recipes!

## Mama's Apple Pie

My mother makes the best apple pie in the world! (I'm aware that I am not the only daughter who makes this claim!) She uses fresh apples, and even after the pie is baked, the apples retain their firm texture and right-off-the-tree flavor. Besides the apple taste, cinnamon is the other dominant note.

Mama has been preparing this well-loved pie for decades. She always flutes the edges of the crust, and uses a

metal heart-shaped cookie cutter to cut valentine-shaped vents
for steam to escape.

* * *

5 c. apples, peeled, cored, and sliced
3/4 c. sugar
2 tbsp. flour
Dash of salt
1 1/2 tsp. cinnamon
2 tbsp. butter
Unbaked double pie crust

Put the sliced apples in the pastry shell.  Mix sugar,
flour, salt, and cinnamon.  Sprinkle over the apples.  Dot
with butter.  Put on the top crust.  Flute edges; make air
vents.  Bake at 350° F. for an hour or until the crust is
golden.

# Saunker Pie

Joan Mitchell Keith, my sister-in-law, has preserved this
heirloom family recipe from southwest Virginia.  Maude
Thomas Helvey, my husband's grandmother, used to serve
this apple cobbler/dumpling type of dessert accompanied by a
pitcher of fresh cream to pour on top.

In Pennsylvania Dutch country, the German word for
this dessert is "schlupper."  In areas of southern Appalachia
(also settled by the Pennsylvania Dutch) schluppers are called
"sonkers" or "sonker pie."  In my husband's family this was
spelled "saunker."

* * *

**Filling:**

1 qt. apples (or peaches), peeled and sliced
1/4 c. sugar
Crushed coriander seed to taste

**Crust:**

3 c. flour
1/2 c. shortening
1/2 tsp. salt

Prepare the filling mixture, and then mix the ingredients for the crust. Using an oblong dish or pan, put the crust in with the excess hanging out over the sides (or use strips of crust fitted along the sides of the pan and hanging down on the outside. These strips are brought up and folded over the top after the filling is put in). Put in the apple mixture and fold over top (or bring up strips of dough). Pinch to seal. Dot with butter and sprinkle with sugar. Bake at 350° F. for about 50 minutes or until apples are tender and crust lightly browned.

Serve in bowls. Pass cream, and if desired, additional sugar for topping.


## Great-Granny's Great Grated Apple Pie

This pie is an old-fashioned favorite . . . . I hope you have an energetic "kitchen assistant" like I do. My 7-year-old son David loves to get out our big, rectangular, boxy-looking metal grater and grate cheese, carrots, apples — anything (thank goodness!).

\* \* \*

2 eggs, well-beaten
1 1/2 c. sugar
1 tsp. lemon juice
1 tsp. apple pie spice
1 tsp. vanilla
1 stick butter or margarine, melted
2 c. peeled and coarsely grated apples
1 unbaked pie shell

Mix the filling ingredients and pour into the pie shell. Bake at 350° F. until the filling is firm.

Not only did this chocolate enthusiast covet the previously mentioned sweets, but I, like hubby Henry, was crazy about pecan clusters. Tootsie Rolls were not bad — for some reason my parents seem to regard them as less of a "treat" than melt-y type candies like Reese's Peanut Butter Cups, Pay Day, Oh! Henry, or Hershey Kisses, so I could eat Tootsie Rolls even when I had not been on my best behavior. (Dad always talked about the advisability of earning "brownie points," but sometimes I earned points on the negative scale . . . .) If I was really "in the doghouse" with the parents (probably deserving to be in the woodshed for a whipping), I was reduced to eating Bit-O-Honey. I did not happen to care for that very stiff, taffy-like confection. Daddy liked it, though. He even loved horehound candy.

Other favorites of mine included Sugar Babies (to eat during regular-length movies) and Sugar Daddies (for epics like *Gone With The Wind*). When I was in elementary school "bricks" of milk chocolate were sold as a fund-raising project. These enormous bars of chocolate temptation were to me like Halloween candy — just too much sheer pig-out pleasure at one shot. I wanted to eat the whole thing at one sitting — very unreasonable. Oh, but they were good . . . .

Chocolate pudding making was my first culinary achievement. Open the box, add the mix to milk in a bowl, beat, chill — instant dessert! (Nice in a pie crust, too, if you wanted to "go gourmet!")

When my facial zits motivated Mom to clamp down on my chocolate consumption (an ill-informed dermatologist stated that lots of foods caused acne; he hadn't learned about blossoming sex hormones . . .), Mom told me to make instant butterscotch pudding, eat Fig Newtons and creme-filled oatmeal cookie "sandwiches" rather than chocolate-chip and fudge ripple cookies, and drink strawberry milkshakes rather than chocolate. I hated the non-chocolate shakes, though the other substitutes were not bad, especially if supplemented with lemon chess pie, A&P Spanish Bar Cake, buttery mints, and peanut butter wafer cookies. — I survived!

# Cousin Lib's Chocolate Angel Pie

Here is a recipe for other chocolate lovers, originally given to me by Mrs. William R. Yeatts of Charlottesville, Virginia.

* * *

3/4 pkg. Nestles semi-sweet chocolate or butterscotch bits
3 tbsp. hot water
1 tsp. vanilla
1/2 pt. cream, whipped
1 baked 8-inch pie shell

Melt bits with hot water over low heat. Add vanilla. Cool. Blend in whipped cream and pour into the pie shell. Chill.

Notes:      This is even more "angelic" if you put the filling into meringue shells.

Chocolate Angel Pie keeps refrigerated two or three days.

# Cheatin' Cherry Pie

This crustless pie is oh-so-easy, and no crust to make (or get home from the grocery store without breaking)!

* * *

1 can cherry pie filling
1 c. milk
1 c. flour
1 c. sugar
1 stick butter

Melt the butter in a pyrex dish. Add the other ingredients, stir, and bake at 350° F. for approximately 40 minutes.

# Georgia Breeze Peach Pie

Peaches are believed to have originated in China, eventually finding their way, through commerce and trade, to Persia (their Latin name is *Prunus persica*, and here *persica* means "Persian"). From Persia (now known as Iran) they went to the Mediterranean, and from there they were among the first "settlers" to put down roots in the New World (as we will see in more detail on the next page).

As a quite young child, I did not realize that canned peaches were the same fruit as fresh peaches (why the name was the same was one of many adult mysteries . . .). The slick canned slices seemed totally different from the fuzzy, fragrant fresh fruit with inner "lipstick" around the pit. — Anyway, Georgia Breeze Peach Pie is an excellent vehicle for the canned product. The cobbler-like treat is swift to fix (truly a breeze!) and especially enjoyable served warm from the oven — yum-yum-euphoric!

\* \* \*

1/4 to 1/2 stick butter or margarine
1/2 c. sugar
1 c. flour (preferably whole wheat)
2 1/2 tsp. baking powder
3/4 c. milk
1 can (29 oz.) sliced peaches

Melt butter in a 13x9x2-inch baking dish. Sift dry ingredients and combine with milk. Pour into the baking dish over the butter. Do not stir! Place peaches and syrup on top. Bake in a 350° F. oven until brown, about 40 minutes.

# Peach Crisp

As early as 322 B. C. the Greeks were enjoying peaches; in first-century Rome the wealthy were paying the equivalent of $4.50 apiece for peaches! Columbus brought peach seeds and trees to America on one or both of his second and third voyages to the New World.

In 1629 the Massachusetts Bay Colony governor ordered peach seeds from Europe. (We Southerners think of the "Persian apple," as they used to be called, as quite "Dixie-ish," but actually peaches can be cultivated almost anywhere that apples grow well!) Peaches were also taken by the English to Jamestown, and by the French to Louisiana. Native Americans loved the new fruit so much that they carried seeds far beyond areas of white settlement. By 1916, 2818 types of peaches were identified. — Peaches had definitely "caught on" in the New World!

Blanket your canned summer fuzz fruits with this topping of sugar and spice and everything nice; bake; and for extra oomph serve with vanilla ice cream.

* * *

1 large can peaches and syrup
1/4 c. brown sugar, packed
1/2 c. whole wheat flour
1/2 c. quick oats, uncooked
1/4 tsp. nutmeg
2 tbsp. butter or margarine, softened
1/4 c. pecans, chopped (optional)

Pour peaches and syrup into a large casserole dish. Mix everything else together until crumbly. Pat the topping over the peaches. Bake uncovered at 350° F. for about 45 minutes.

# Impossible Coconut Pie

### (Makes its own crust!)

Talking about desserts, I can especially remember my delight and astonishment as a young girl at my first encounter with a restaurant dessert cart. Surely this was a temptation devised by Santa Claus, Walt Disney, and Betty Crocker! Beautiful red fruited Jello layered with whipped cream in graceful parfait glasses (the likes of which I had never seen before — the tall vase-like glasses, not the Jello); mysterious dark, chocolatey-looking pecan pie; luscious lemon and chocolate meringue pies; wedges of peach pie with peachy syrup oozing out of the crust; lattice-topped pies (also new to me); unusual coconut/pineapple multilayered cakes; deep brown, shiny, glistening chocolate icing crowning rich chocolate cake; dainty tarts; and often a bowl of ambrosia. How could one choose? Go with something you recognize? Try something new you might not like? Ask for Mom's advice? Order ice cream instead? — What a wonderful dilemma!

Coconut pie is an old dessert-cart favorite, and this version does indeed produce its own "crust" while baking.

\* \* \*

4 eggs
2 c. milk
1 tsp. vanilla
1/2 c. self-rising flour
1 1/2 c. sugar
1/2 stick butter, melted
2 2/3 c. coconut

Mix all ingredients and pour into two greased 9-inch pie pans. Bake at 350° F. for 30-40 minutes.

# Pecan Pies

Spanish explorers traveling through Texas during the 1500's reported that Indians ate pecans to ward off starvation. Eating these pies definitely has the same result!

\* \* \*

### Home-Style Pecan Pie

3/4 c. dark Karo syrup
1/2 c. sugar
1/4 c. butter, melted

2 large eggs, slightly beaten
1 tsp. vanilla
1/2 c. pecans, chopped
1  9-inch unbaked pie shell

Combine the first six ingredients and pour into the pie shell.  Bake at 350° F. for 30 to 40 minutes (until the crust is nicely browned).

## Fancy Pecan Pie

1/2 c. butter, melted
3 eggs, beaten
1 c. sugar
Dash of salt
1 tsp. vanilla
1 c. white Karo syrup
1 c. pecans, chopped
1  9-inch unbaked pie shell

Mix all ingredients well, adding pecans last.  Pour into an unbaked pie shell and bake at 350° F. for 30 minutes or until brown.  The pecans will come to the top of the pie.

\* \* \*

Note:  Jane Irby of Fredericksburg, Virginia, offers the following smart tip to use when making pecan pies.  Separate out a little egg white before beating the eggs and mixing with the other ingredients.  Beat this small amount of egg white and spread over the unbaked crust.  Add filling and bake as usual.  — The egg white prevents the crust from becoming soggy/gummy.

# Lemon Chess Pie

Lemon Chess Pie, consisting of a sweet-tart translucent filling baked in a plain pastry shell, is an old Virginia favorite.

However, the word "chess" is rather mystifying. One oft-heard explanation is that folks used to keep these pies in their pie safe, a tin-and-wooden upright chest with shelves for storing baked goods. (There was no refrigeration, of course. The pies were merely locked away to protect them from hungry varmints, human and otherwise.) Anyway, the pies were kept in a chest, and people with soft Southern drawls called this piece of furniture a "ches'." Eventually, according to this explanation, the pie stored in this "ches'" came to be known as Lemon Chess Pie.

In more scholarly (and probably more accurate) discussion of the "chess" topic, Southern food expert Bill Neal asserts in his *Biscuits, Spoonbread, and Sweet Potato Pie* (Alfred A. Knopf, 1990): "The name is a corruption of cheese, for in the British culinary tradition eggs and cheese share the same terminology . . . ."

\* \* \*

1/4 c. butter
1 1/2 c. sugar
1 tbsp. flour
3 eggs
Juice of 1 1/2 lemons (should equal 1/3 cup)
1  9-inch unbaked pastry shell

Thoroughly cream butter and sugar with an electric mixer. Stir in flour. Then add eggs, one at a time. Next add lemon juice and mix well. Pour into the pastry shell and bake for 15 minutes at 375° F., then reduce heat to 300° F. and bake an additional 40 minutes.

## Southern Surprise Lemon Pies

At Brennan's famous French Quarter restaurant in New Orleans, Maude's Peanut Butter Pie is an oft-ordered dessert, so do not be surprised at the suggestion of peanut butter in pie — it's great! Whip up the following recipe — *Bon appétit!*

2 8-inch graham cracker pie shells or 24 mini-pie shells
3 oz. cream cheese, at room temperature
2 tbsp. milk
1 c. confectioner's sugar, sifted
1 c. crunchy peanut butter

Cream the cheese and milk together, using an electric mixer. Blend in sugar. Add peanut butter, beating at medium speed. Divide mixture in half and press into the two pie shells, or put 1 tbsp. of mixture into each mini shell.

**Filling:**

8 oz. cream cheese
1 14-oz. can sweetened condensed milk
1/3 c. lemon juice
1 can lemon pie filling, or 3 3/8 oz. lemon pudding and pie
    filling prepared according to package directions
1 tsp. vanilla
1/2 c. peanuts, chopped

Cream the cheese. Add condensed milk. Blend in mixer. Add lemon juice and beat until mixture begins to thicken. Blend in pie filling and vanilla. Spoon into pie shells. Top with chopped peanuts. Refrigerate.

# Southland Spring Fresh Strawberry Pie

Red and shimmery, Southland Spring Fresh Strawberry Pie is a real pleasure-giver. This dessert was introduced to us by our friend Helen Melton of Hillsville, Virginia. Shoney's Restaurants serve a popular commercial version of this recipe.

* * *

1 c. sugar
3 tbsp. cornstarch

1 c. water
3 tbsp. strawberry-flavored Jello
2 c. strawberries
1 9-inch baked pastry shell
Whipped cream or whipped dessert topping

Mix sugar and cornstarch in a saucepan, and add water. Cook until mixture is thick and clear. Add strawberry-flavored Jello powder and mix well. Put clean, hulled strawberries into a baked pastry shell, and pour mixture over the berries. Top with whipped cream or whipped dessert topping.


## Mom's Strawberry-Banana Pie

Oriental chefs are known for their exquisitely beautiful presentation of food. A meal in the Far East may become an artistic masterpiece of color, balance, taste, and texture — each plate arranged to create a harmonious "still life." My mother has studied Oriental techniques of flower arranging. Perhaps that knowledge carried over into her cooking, because her meals "are," she sometimes laughs, "too pretty to eat!" (But we manage to, happily!)

Mom developed this recipe in which strawberries and bananas team up in a lovely, not-too-sweet, non-exotic pie. (Appropriately, strawberries are plants of the rose family.)

* * *

1 pkg. frozen strawberries
2 tbsp. cornstarch
2 tbsp. water
1 tbsp. lemon juice
1 envelope unflavored gelatin
1/4 c. cold water
1 banana
1 graham cracker crumb crust

Drain frozen strawberries. Set aside. Mix the juice from the berries with the 2 tbsp. cornstarch and 2 tbsp. water.

Cook together the liquid mixture until translucent. Soften together 1 tbsp. lemon juice, gelatin, and 1/4 c. cold water. Combine with warm juice mixture. Fold in drained strawberries and sliced banana. Pour into crust. Chill.

# Tricia's Cheese Cake

The "parent recipe" for this one came from Peg Bracken, writer of *The I Hate to Cook Book* and the *Appendix to the I Hate to Cook Book*. I enjoyed her humorous cookbooks (even though I *love* to cook) because her recipes are uncomplicated and unpretentious. Try this delicate, easy-to-make cheese cake. You will be glad Peg cooked, whether she liked it or not!

* * *

2 small packages cream cheese
1/3 c. sugar
1/2 tsp. vanilla
1 egg, slightly beaten
1 9-inch graham cracker crumb crust
1 c. sour cream

Cream together cream cheese, sugar, vanilla, and egg. Put into the crumb crust and bake at 325° F. for 20 minutes. Hike the oven up to 450° F., spread a cup of sour cream all over the top of the pie, sprinkle a tablespoon of sugar on that, and bake it for 5 minutes.

Note: For a less "fatty" dessert, substitute mock sour cream for the dairy sour cream. Make "mock" this way: In a blender combine 1 c. cottage cheese and 1 tbsp. lemon juice. Blend until smooth.

# Daddy's Dessert

My father had a severe heart attack in 1959, but lived another 21 years after that. Mom had to learn to cook differently following his first attack. This light dessert is a recipe I prepared for him.

* * *

1 small can crushed pineapple
1 small box lemon jello
1/3 c. instant nonfat dry milk powder
1 c. cottage cheese
1 1/2 c. graham cracker crumbs

Thoroughly drain the pineapple, reserving the juice. To the juice add enough water to equal 1 cup. Heat the liquid to the boiling point. Stir in the jello and chill until slightly thickened. Sprinkle dry milk powder over jello. Beat at high speed with an electric mixer until the mixture is thick and doubled in bulk. Fold in cottage cheese and pineapple. Spread half of the graham cracker crumbs in a 9x9-inch pan. Alternate layers of pineapple/cheese mixture with remaining crumbs. Chill at least 2 hours before serving.

## Creamy Pumpkin Pie

What could be more American than apple pie? Pumpkin pie, of course! Pumpkin pie is an American "invention," although it is an offshoot of English custard pie. Early settlers to this continent experimented with native foods, developing, among other things, recipes for pumpkin bread and pumpkin pie. Often they used molasses or maple syrup in their pumpkin pies when sugar was unavailable.

Who could imagine Thanksgiving and/or Christmas holiday diners without pumpkin pie? The following recipe is our favorite.

* * *

2 c. canned pumpkin
1 14-oz. can condensed milk (Here's where the sweetening is hidden!)

2 eggs, beaten
1 tsp. cinnamon
1/2 tsp. *each* of salt, ginger, and nutmeg
1 unbaked pie shell

Mix the pie ingredients well and pour into the shell. Bake at 425° F. for 15 minutes and reduce heat to 350° F. Bake for 35 additional minutes, checking to see that it does not get too brown.

## Cousin Wanda's Pumpkin Roll

The perfect holiday dessert, this impressive cake (sort of a sophisticated jelly roll) will wow your friends and family! My cousin Wanda Carter of Morganton, North Carolina, gave me the instructions.

\* \* \*

3 eggs
1 c. sugar
2/3 c. canned pumpkin
1 tsp. lemon juice
3/4 c. flour
1 tsp. baking powder
1/2 tsp. salt
2 tsp. cinnamon
1 tsp. ginger
1/2 tsp. nutmeg
1 c. nuts, chopped

Beat the eggs with an electric mixer on high speed for 5 minutes. Gradually beat in sugar. Stir in pumpkin and lemon juice. Sift together the dry ingredients (excluding the nuts) and fold into pumpkin mixture. Spread batter in a greased and floured 15x10x1-inch pan. Sprinkle on nuts. Bake at 375° F. for 15 minutes. After removing from oven, turn out on a clean dish towel sprinkled well with powdered sugar. Roll the cake and towel together. Cool, unroll.

**Filling for Pumpkin Roll:**

1 c. powdered sugar
1 3-oz. pkg. cream cheese
1/4 c. butter
1/2 tsp. vanilla
1/2 c. whipped dessert topping

Combine and beat until smooth. Spread on cool unrolled cake; roll again; chill; slice.

# Big Jerp-uh-'Lasses Oatmeal Cake

Old-timers in the mountains call a small amount or quantity of something sweet (like molasses or honey) a "jerp." So put a big "jerp" of molasses in the following moist and spice-laced cake.

\* \* \*

1 1/2 c. boiling water
1 c. quick-cooking oats
1/2 c. vegetable oil
3/4 c. molasses
1/4 c. sugar
2 eggs, beaten
1 1/4 c. flour (all-purpose, unbleached, or whole wheat)
1 tsp. soda
1 tsp. baking powder
1/2 tsp. salt
1/2 tsp. cinnamon
1/2 tsp. ginger
1/4 tsp. cloves
1/4 tsp. nutmeg

Pour boiling water over oats. Stir and let sit 20 minutes. In a different bowl, combine oil, molasses, sugar, and eggs. Stir in oats mixture. Sift dry ingredients, and gradually add to wet mixture. Combine thoroughly. Pour batter into a greased 13x9-inch baking pan. Bake at 350° F.

for 25-30 minutes. Serve warm or cold with lemon sauce (see recipe on page 36).

# Heirloom Spicy Gingerbread

Gingerbread, first recorded in medieval English manuscripts as a medicinal concoction, in time became a folk art form, with edible and inedible (gold leaf-covered) examples in elaborate and fanciful shapes and figures sold from gaily-decorated booths at English fairs. Gingerbread came across the Atlantic early on. It is said to have been a favorite of George Washington.

After years of experimentation and tasting, our family has agreed on this recipe as our first choice.

\* \* \*

2 c. whole wheat flour
1 1/2 tsp. baking soda
1/2 tsp. salt
2 1/2 tsp. ginger
1 1/2 tsp. cinnamon
1/2 tsp. cloves
1/2 c. butter or other shortening
1/2 c. brown sugar
2 eggs, beaten until stiff
3/4 c. molasses
1 c. boiling water

Sift together the first six ingredients. Set aside. Cream the butter and add sugar, beating unti light and fluffy. Add the eggs.

Blend in 1/4 of the dry ingredients. Add the molasses, beating until smooth. Then add remaining dry ingredients, beating well. Stir in boiling water.

Pour into a greased 9x13x2-inch glass dish and bake approximately 40 minutes at 350° F.

# Jackson Square Cake

Come, let's take an imaginary trip, down the mighty Mississip', to the enticing city of New Orleans. — In the heart of the *Vieux Carré* (the French Quarter), Jackson Square sizzles with activity. From it radiates the life of the Quarter — the French Market, selling its delicious fruits and vegetables, the spice shop, the confection shop, all the gourmet stops for the French Quarter resident to fill her "shopping basket." Get your Louisiana brown sugar, your aromatic spices, your fresh pecans, the raisins and chocolate bits, then bake up this surprising delight!

* * *

1 c. boiling water
1 c. regular oats, uncooked
1/4 c. butter or margarine, softened
1 c. brown sugar, packed
2 eggs
1 c. whole wheat flour
1 tsp. soda
Dash of salt
1 tsp. cinnamon
1/2 tsp. nutmeg
1/2 tsp. cloves
1 c. pecans, chopped
1/2 c. raisins
1/2 c. semisweet chocolate morsels or carob chips

Combine water and oats in a small bowl. Let stand 15 minutes. Cream butter and sugar in a large bowl. Add eggs, beating well. Beat in next 6 ingredients. Add oats mixture. Stir thoroughly. Mix in last 3 ingredients. Pour batter into a greased 8-inch square baking pan and bake at 350° F. for about 30 minutes.


# Carob-Oat Cake

Over the years we have become more health-conscious. This is a delicious, guilt-free dessert.

2 1/2 c. boiling water
1 c. oats
1/4 c. vegetable oil
2/3 c. brown sugar
2 tsp. vanilla
2/3 c. carob

1 1/2 c. whole wheat flour
1 tsp. baking powder
1 tsp. soda
1/2 tsp. salt

Combine the first six ingredients, stirring well. In a separate bowl mix the remaining ingredients. Stir together the two mixtures, and pour the batter into a greased 8-inch square baking pan. Bake at 350° F. for 30 minutes.

Carob-Oat Cake is especially nice served with warm **Whisper 'o' Honey Glaze:**

1 c. milk
4 tsp. cornstarch
1/4 c. honey

In a small saucepan blend together the three ingredients. Slowly cook over low-to-medium heat until thickened. (Do not boil.)

# Stolen Sweetness Banana Coffee Cake

When he was a lad, my Uncle Jake once stole a banana from the local country store. Immediately thereafter, my grandfather bought a Gargantuan bunch of bananas (a bunch as tall as a boy), hung it in the kitchen, and required that the offender eat bananas *very frequently* to prove to himself that he did not have to steal to get what he wanted. Funny thing, Uncle Jake still loves bananas . . .

Now *purchase* some bananas and bake this fabulous cake!

*Read complete instructions before proceeding!*

1/2 c. butter or margarine
2/3 c. sugar
1 3/4 c. whole wheat flour
2 tsp. baking powder
1/2 tsp. salt
1/2 tsp. cinnamon
1/4 tsp. baking soda
2 eggs, beaten
1 c. mashed bananas ( 2 ripe bananas)
3/4 c. milk
1 tsp. vanilla

Cream butter and sugar. Add 3/4 c. of the flour. Mix until crumbly. Set aside 1/2 c. of this mixture for topping. Sift together remaining 1 c. flour, baking powder, salt, cinnamon, and soda. Add to butter mixture. Combine moist ingredients and blend into dry mixture. Spread in a greased 9x9x2-inch baking pan. Sprinkle with reserved topping, and gently pat down the topping. Bake at 375° F. for 20-30 minutes.

# Carolina Prune Cake

Everyone likes a good, tasty, take-along kind of cake recipe for covered-dish suppers or at-home entertaining. Carolina Prune Cake keeps well and freezes nicely, too. Janette Forbes Beaver, my aunt in Charlotte, North Carolina, gave me this recipe, which I modified just slightly.

* * *

2 c. flour, plain or whole wheat
1 tsp. cinnamon
1 tsp. nutmeg
1 tsp. allspice
1 tsp. soda
1 1/2 c. sugar

3 eggs
1 c. Wesson or vegetable oil
1 c. buttermilk
1 c. pecans or walnuts, chopped
1/2 c. coconut, shredded
1 tsp. vanilla
1 c. cooked prunes, pitted and chopped

Sift together flour, cinnamon, nutmeg, allspice, soda, and sugar. In a separate bowl beat together eggs, oil, and buttermilk. Mix the dry ingredients into the wet mixture. Then add nuts, coconut, vanilla, and prunes. Pour into a greased tube or bundt pan. Bake at 325° F. for one hour.

**Buttermilk Icing for Carolina Prune Cake:**

1/3 c. sugar
1/2 tbsp. corn syrup
2 tbsp. butter
1/4 c. buttermilk
1/4 tsp. soda
1/4 tsp. vanilla

Mix in a saucepan, stirring until sugar is dissolved. Pour over baked cake.

# Church Supper Brown Sugar Pound Cake

Thank goodness for electric mixers! Old recipes for pound cake direct the cook to beat the batter for one *hour* by hand!

One popular cookbook writer of the mid-1700's, Mrs. Hannah Glasse, made her pound cake with a pound each of butter, sugar, and flour; one dozen egg yolks and half a dozen whites; and a pound of currants or caraway seeds (!!!) for seasoning.

Arlene Brumfield charmed our hometown church gatherings with this recipe many years ago. Be sure to try it — no caraway seeds, please, although I know some adults who like to eat bread 'n' butter pickles with pound cake!

* * *

1/2 lb. butter or margarine
1/2 c. Crisco shortening
5 eggs
1 c. sweet milk
3 1/2 c. all-purpose flour
1 1/2 tsp. vanilla
1/2 tsp. baking powder
1 box brown sugar
1 c. white sugar

Cream butter and Crisco shortening together until fluffy. Add sugar, one cup at a time, and cream thoroughly. Add eggs, one at a time, and beat thoroughly after each addition. Sift flour and measure, then sift flour and baking powder together. Add dry ingredients and milk alternately into the creamed mixture. When thoroughly mixed, add vanilla. Pour into a well-greased and floured tube pan. Bake at 325° F. for 1 1/2 hours.

# Rascal Rabbit Carrot Cake

Carrots are thought to have been grown first in the Orient. They were introduced into England during the reign of Elizabeth I. The root vegetable was brought to the colonies (that's us!) in the 1600's.

We know today that carrots are high in carotene (which in the body helps to form vitamin A) and that the fiber in carrots is bile-binding.

When you bake this cake, be prepared to deal with (in Elmer Fudd's terminology) all those "wascal wabbits" in your household who "can't stay away from the cawwot cake!"

* * *

1 1/2 c. sugar
3 egg yolks
1 c. vegetable oil
5 1/2 tbsp. hot water
1 1/2 c. flour
1 tsp. baking powder
1/2 tsp. soda
Pinch of salt
1/2 tsp. cinnamon
1/4 tsp. nutmeg
1 c. raw carrots, grated
1 c. black walnuts, chopped
3 egg whites, beaten until fluffy

Combine the first four ingredients and beat 200 strokes. Add the remaining things, except for the egg whites, which you fold in last. Pour into a greased cake pan lined on the bottom with waxed paper. Bake at 350° F. for 55 minutes.

## Chattanooga Applesauce Layer Cake

During the late 1970's my family and I attended a Christian fellowship at Ringgold, Virginia. After the Sunday service, we often had a pot-luck lunch, with the ladies all bringing food. One Sunday Nancy Tipton Gosney brought this moist, brimming-with-sweetness cake. The heirloom recipe was from her Grandmother Higdon of Chattanooga, Tennessee. This cake is an old-fashioned, deliciously heavy cake, not one of your modern "light as a feather" (full of air) cakes.

* * *

2 c. sugar
2/3 c. butter
2/3 c. raisins, ground up in blender
2 1/2 c. *hot* applesauce
4 c. all-purpose flour, sifted
4 tsp. baking soda
2 tsp. cinnamon
1 tsp. ground cloves

Cream together the sugar and butter. Add blender-chopped raisins and hot applesauce. Sift together the dry ingredients, and add to the first mixture. Pour into three prepared round cake pans, and bake at 350° F. for 30 minutes.

Meanwhile, put 4 c. brown sugar, 2 c. milk, and an egg-sized lump of butter in a saucepan. Stir constantly. (If it curdles or becomes lumpy, beat with a rotary egg beater.) Cook to the soft ball stage. Remove from burner, and beat fast while it cools. Add 1 tsp. vanilla, and beat some more.

After removing cooled cake layers from pans, pour filling over each layer and stack.

## Chocolate Walnut Cookies

When Henry was stationed at the Defense Electronics Supply Center in Dayton, Ohio, we lived near a walnut tree. (Trees make nice neighbors, especially nut- or fruit-bearing varieties!) Here in Chatham, we have several walnut trees. Thus blessed, I have tried many walnut recipes.

Put walnuts and chocolate together with some other baking ingredients and you can produce mighty fine morsels. — As you know, chocolate is one of America's favorite flavors. It has a history here that goes 'way back to 1764 when young Irish immigrant chocolate-maker John Hannon complained to prosperous Dr. James Baker that there was no chocolate mill in the New World. The (presumably chocolate-loving) doctor set Hannon up in business — providing capital; leasing a mill on the banks of the Neponset River in Dorcester, Massachusetts; and obtaining millstones and kettles — the rest is history, as they say. (You've heard of Baker's Chocolate, *n'est-ce pas?*) Very soon, chocolate figuratively ran down across America, all the way to the Gulf of Mexico!

* * *

1/2 c. margarine
1 c. sugar

2 eggs, well-beaten
2 squares semi-sweet chocolate, melted
1 c. walnuts, chopped
1/4 tsp. salt
1/4 tsp. vanilla
2/3 c. flour

Cream margarine. Beat in sugar. Add other ingredients. Drop large tablespoons of dough on a greased cookie sheet. Bake at 400° F. for 12 minutes.

# Dr. Feelgood's Oatmeal Cookies

Nutritionists, dedicated to helping us "feel good," applaud oats. The water-soluble fiber in oats lowers cholesterol levels; and the "bulk" or "roughage" (as grandmother used to call it) in oats make them stick-to-the-ribs-fillin' and satisfyin'. If you get tired of oatmeal for breakfast, these "crumb-snatching good" cookies make a novel change!

I've already described my early years as a thoroughgoing chocolate freak and sugar "seducee." (Even Girl Scout cookies made a suitable snack orgy.) *Any* batch of cookies was likely to get devoured by this indiscriminate sugar craver. A little girl friend of mine (much more dainty than I) liked the flat, donut-shaped buttery vanilla cookies in the Nabisco assortment. When together, she and I stuck the circular cookies on our little fingers and nibbled around and around — "finger food!"

* * *

1/2 c. margarine
1 c. sugar
1 egg, beaten
1/2 tsp. soda dissolved in 1 tbsp. water
1/2 tsp. salt
1 1/4 c. flour
1 1/4 c. quick oats, uncooked
1/2 c. raisins coated with 1 tbsp. flour

Cream together margarine and sugar. Add everything else and mix thoroughly. Place rounded tablespoons of dough on an ungreased cookie sheet. Leave plenty of space between the mounds of cookie dough because they flatten out and get big. Bake at 425° F. for about 7 minutes, then turn on the broiler unit for a minute or two until the tops of the cookies are lightly brown.

## Big Top Spice Cookies

The reason that these cookies are especially delicious is their mammoth size. Do not bake them as petite 1 1/2"-diameter things! Make them vast! 2 1/2" in diameter is something you can sink your teeth into! Instead of having to eat half a dozen cookies to satisfy yourself, you can be satiated after devouring only a few. Another advantage of giant cookies is that the spiciness and texture seem to be more pronounced when you have a generous sample.

* * *

3/4 shortening or 1/2 c. vegetable oil
1 c. sugar or 1/2 c. honey (If sugar is used,
     add enough water to moisten.)
1 egg
1/4 c. molasses
2 c. flour, preferably whole wheat
2 tsp. soda
1/4 tsp. salt
1 tsp. cinnamon
3/4 tsp. ginger
1/2 tsp. cloves

Mix together shortening, sugar, egg, and molasses. Stir in dry ingredients, and form dough into walnut-sized balls. Flatten out and place on an ungreased cookie sheet. Bake at 375° F. for 10 minutes, then slightly brown the tops of the cookies by turning on the broiler for a minute or two.

# Lemon Raisin Drops

This recipe makes a small batch of cookies *fast* and easy. This one is from our early married days . . . .

* * *

1/2 c. butter or margarine
3/4 c. sugar
1 egg
2 tbsp. milk
1/2 tsp. lemon extract
1 3/4 c. self-rising flour
1/2 c. raisins

Cream together the butter and sugar; beat in egg, milk, and extract. Stir in flour and raisins. Drop mounds onto a greased cookie sheet. Bake at 400° F. for 10-12 minutes.


# Market Squares

This tempting bar cookie is named in honor of Charleston, South Carolina's market area. The cookie recipe is a chewy mixture of prunes, pecans, oats, and other basic "cookie materials."

* * *

**Filling:**

1 pkg. (12 oz.) pitted prunes, chopped
    (2 c. cooked, pitted prunes)
1 1/2 c. water
1/4 c. packed dark brown sugar
1/4 c. whole wheat flour
1 tbsp. lemon juice
1/2 tsp. ground ginger

**Crust:**

1 1/2 c. whole wheat flour
1 1/2 c. quick oats, uncooked

2/3 c. dark brown sugar, packed
1/2 c. pecans, chopped
3/4 tsp. salt
3/4 c. butter or margarine, melted

*Filling:* In medium-sized saucepan combine prunes and water. Cover and simmer 15 minutes. Beat in sugar, flour, lemon juice, and ginger. Let cool.

*Crust and assembly:* Grease a 9x13x3-inch pan. In a large bowl combine flour, oats, sugar, pecans, and salt. Stir in butter or margarine. Reserving 1 c. for top, pat remaining crumbs into pan. Spread prune filling to within 1/2" of edges. Sprinkle with reserved crumbs. Bake 25-30 minutes at 350° F. or until edges are browned. Cool on a wire rack.

# Marse Tom's Delight Butterscotch Brownies

Pecans were brought to the East Coast by none other than Thomas Jefferson, who moved some trees from the Mississippi Valley to Monticello, his home in Virginia. He gave a few trees to George Washington, who planted them at Mount Vernon. It is said that three of those original trees still exist at Mount Vernon.

The shape of pecans varies from egg-shaped oval to quite elongated. Some varieties include Major, Burkett, Warrick, Ravens, and Owens. Pecan trees begin to bear well when they are about 20 years old; and are an important food crop in the South. (Pecan wood is also used in furniture — for example, the chair in which I am seated as I write this.)

The state of Georgia leads the world in the production of paper shell pecans, the most popular type because you can literally crush the shell between your fingers.

So get cracking, and bake up some soft and full-bodied "blond" brownies!

\* \* \*

1/4 c. whole wheat flour
1/3 c. wheat germ
1/2 c. nonfat dry milk powder
1/4 tsp. salt
1/2 c. pecans, chopped
1/2 c. brown sugar
2 eggs, beaten
2 tbsp. vegetable oil
1 tbsp. molasses

Mix ingredients in the given order. Spoon into a greased 9x9-inch pan. Bake at 325° F. for 20 minutes. Cool and serve cut into squares.

## Chocolate / Peanut Butter Brownies

Remember the amusing scene in *Gone With the Wind* in which Rhett has taken Scarlett to New Orleans after the War? They are dining, and Scarlett is literally stuffing her face with cakes and pastries, washing it down with wine, and simultaneously pointing to more goodies she wants from the waiter's tray. She would have loved these treats!

Of course, at the supposed time of Scarlett's New Orleans feast George Washington Carver was still a little boy. The South would have to wait for him to grow up to become the great agricultural scientist and promoter of crops which could help renew the South's cotton-depleted soil. By the time Carver finished his crusade, peanuts were more "Southern" than King Cotton himself!

In this recipe the chocolate taste is dominant; the peanut butter just adds nuts and moistness, making the brownies chewy and sticky, similar to fudge.

* * *

1/4 c. butter or margarine
2 squares (2 oz.) unsweetened chocolate

3/4 c. sugar
1/4 c. crunchy peanut butter
1/4 tsp. salt
1/2 tsp. vanilla
2 eggs
1/2 c. flour

Melt butter and chocolate together over low heat. Cool. Add sugar, peanut butter, salt, and vanilla. Beat in eggs. Blend in flour. Pour into a greased 8x8x2-inch pan. Bake at 350° F. for 20 minutes. — These brownies freeze well.

## Sweet Beaver Fudge

The first time I made fudge, when I was a Brownie Scout (a Fudge Scout?), the troop leader instructed us to bring a bowl, spoon, and pan to our regular Wednesday afternoon meeting in the Chatham Presbyterian Church basement. Our job would be to help with the fudge preparation, and take home a batch. We gathered in the church kitchen, where the fudge ingredients were assembled. I had purchased a turquoise bowl and matching plastic spoon. (Mom still has the bowl.) When my turn came to stir the hot fudge mixture on the stove, I had only stirred briefly when I discovered that my beauteous turquoise spoon had softened into an unusual spiral!

Meanwhile, Cousin Wanda Beaver (now Carter) was in North Carolina and apparently earning A's in fudgemaking while I was merely melting spoons. Wanda had the clever idea of basing this recipe on a favorite frosting recipe. How could such rich essence of chocolate be concentrated in a fudge?! Tastes so good it'll make your teeth sing!

* * *

1 stick margarine
4-5 tbsp. milk
1/4 c. cocoa
1 tsp. vanilla

1 box confectioner's sugar
3 tbsp. peanut butter (optional)
1/2 c. chopped nuts (optional)

Mix ingredients, except sugar, in a saucepan. Bring to a boil. Pour into a bowl containing the powdered sugar. Mix. Spread into a greased square or rectangular pan. Press down to make the top of the fudge level. Chill. Cut into squares to serve.

# Prodigal Fudge

In the Biblical account of the Prodigal Son, the wayward youth goes to a foreign land and squanders his share of his father's money. The young man is reduced to feeding husks to swine. Those "husks" were carob pods! Too bad he did not grind those pods into carob powder, and make this superspectacular fudge! (Of course, then the story would not be so instructive.)

This healthful recipe tastes extraordinary — rich, chocolate-like, and creamy! Wow!! A sure-fire favorite (and no cooking involved). Sarah, Henry, and David often ask me to fix this for their birthdays, rather than cake. (I make a double batch in a 9x13x2-inch pyrex dish, topped with candles.)

* * *

1/4 c. margarine
1 1/3 c. nonfat dry milk powder
2/3 c. carob powder
1/3 c. honey
2 tsp. vanilla
1-2 tbsp. water (optional)
1 c. sunflower seeds

Using an electric mixer, beat together the margarine and dry milk powder. Add carob powder, honey, and vanilla. Beat until smooth, adding a tbsp. or two of water if the mixture is too thick. Fold in sunflower seeds. Pat into an 8-inch square pan, or form into a roll in plastic wrap, and chill. To serve, cut in squares or round slices.

# Memories-Are-Made-of Strawberry Sweets

Everybody has "nostalgia" foods. Many nostalgia foods are "comfort foods," i.e., foods that produce a particularly positive psychological effect when consumed — usually because of happy memories with which they are connected. Perhaps when you accomplish something special, you reward yourself with a slice of German chocolate cake because your beloved grandmother often served that dessert to you; or when you feel pressured and/or depressed, you eat a Baby Ruth candy bar or buy a bag of popcorn because as a child those goodies were "save-up-the-allowance" treats for you.

Strawberry sweets are a memory food for me. When I was a little girl, Mother made these dainties to serve at bridge club parties or at garden club meetings. — I was quite amazed at her skill in creating such pretty (imitation) berries! And their taste! Oh, my, so wonderfully sugar-sweet! The very recollection of these red tidbits on a silver or crystal serving plate brings moistness to my eyes — I see myself as an innocent, carefree child then — a bygone era.

\* \* \*

1/2 c. butter, melted
2 eggs, beaten
1 c. sugar
8 oz. pkg. dates, minced finely
1/2 c. flour
Red food coloring

Partially melt butter. Add eggs and sugar. Mix. Blend in dates. Cook 5 minutes over low heat, stirring constantly. Add flour gradually. Cook, stirring, until thick, 7 to 10 minutes. Add red food coloring, blending throughout. Form into strawberry shapes.

# Mom's World-Class Banana Pudding

Bananas are the best-selling fruit in the United States, even if you count only the popular Gros Michel or Martinique banana and not the larger plantain sold in Louisiana and used primarily as a cooked vegetable.

Our bananas are grown in hot, damp Central America on 10- to 25-foot-high plants (not really trees) which reach maturity in only 12-15 months. Conveniently for man and monkey, banana peels are dirt- and germ-proof; and, as you know, the pulp is luscious. Make a bowl of my Mom's World-Class Banana Pudding and enjoy!

* * *

3 or 4 ripe bananas, sliced
1 box of vanilla wafers
2 1/2 c. milk
3 tbsp. cornstarch
1/4 tsp. salt
3 egg yolks, beaten
1 tsp. vanilla extract
3 egg whites
6 tbsp. sugar

In a pyrex dish make alternating layers of bananas and wafers. (You may not use all the wafers.) Meanwhile, put cornstarch in a bit of the milk and blend. Now put this liquid, along with the rest of the milk, into a saucepan. Add salt. Heat, stirring until thickened. Put several spoonfuls of that milk mixture into a cup with 3 egg yolks, and then gradually add to the hot mixture on the stove. Add vanilla. Stir well. Pour this hot liquid over the bananas and wafers. Next beat the egg whites with 6 tbsp. sugar to form meringue. Spread meringue over the pudding and brown lightly in a 350° F. oven. Serve at room temperature or chilled.

# Encore Bread Pudding

The French bread in New Orleans is too good to waste, so *Pain Perdu* ("Lost Bread" or French toast) is a popular dish there, as is bread pudding. This practical and tasty dessert is gratifying served hot or cold in Louisiana or elsewhere. It will make you hope for leftover bread (whole wheat is especially good). At our house, everyone always wants second helpings of Encore Bread Pudding!

2 c. milk
4 c. bread crumbs
1/4 c. butter or margarine, melted
2 eggs, beaten
1/3 c. sugar
1/4 tsp. salt
1 tsp. cinnamon
1/2 c. raisins

Mix all ingredients and spoon into a 1 1/2-quart casserole dish. Bake 40-50 minutes at 350° F. Serve with the following sauce.

**Lemon Sauce:**

1/3 c. sugar
2 tbsp. cornstarch
1/8 tsp. salt
1 c. water
2 tsp. grated lemon peel (optional)
1/3 c. lemon juice
1 tbsp. butter or margarine

Combine the first four ingredients, and cook until thickened, stirring frequently. Add the remaining ingredients. Stir and heat. Reduce heat and cover until ready to serve. Yield: approximately 1 1/3 cups.

# Conclusion

This cookbook runs the gamut from sugary sensations to fairly health-conscious desserts — something for everyone. Remember, desserts especially tend to be comfort foods, their psychological benefits frequently outweighing their nutritional merit. . . . We humans are spirits. We have a soul, and we live in a body. Sometimes the body and soul need a bit of pleasure. — Don't you and your family deserve a simply scrumptious dessert today?!